Fugitive but Gorgeous

Poems

Elinor Ann Walker

Sheila-Na-Gig Editions

Cover photo: Elinor Ann Walker
Author photo: Will Phillips

ISBN: 978-1-962405-62-1

Sheila-Na-Gig Editions
Russell, KY
Hayley Mitchell Haugen, Editor
www.sheilanagigblog.com

Acknowledgments

With many thanks to the editors, publishers, composers, and readers of the following venues in which these works previously appeared, some in different versions:

2024 LMNL Anthology (LMNL Arts, 2025): “Matters as Simple as Quantum Mechanics,” semifinalist for the 2024 Patty Friedmann Writing Contest for Poetry
AGNI: “Pantoum Composed of Lines After Paintings of Girls”
Bear Review: “Mapping”
Bracken: “Haunt Like This”
Dark Confessions (Black Bough Poetry, 2021): “Dizzy”
Fantastic, Imaginary Creatures: An Anthology of Contemporary Prose Poems (Madville Publishing, 2024): “Fugue State”
Fevers of the Mind: "Baby Teeth" (reprint)
Glimpses of Grief and Glee, a concert of original chamber music: “Clef” (as “Triple Clef”), which was commissioned for this performance in Birmingham, AL.
Gone Lawn: “Undomesticated Ghosts”
Gyroscope Review: “Lioness”
Jet Fuel Review: “Fugue State,” “Song for Cello & Girlhood”
MacQueen's Quinterly: “Fugitive but Gorgeous,” “Polymorphous Pigeon in the Art Museum”
Mom Egg Review: “I will hunger”
Naugatuck River Review: “Geminids, Field Report”
Orca: “After the Anniversary Party for the Feathery Woman & Blindfolded Man,” “Through a Quantum Flute,” “You Only Ghosted Me in Your Head”
Painted Pebble Lit Mag: “How Lost Words Haunt Like Wings Behind Glass”
perhappened mag: “Driving Rain”
Pidgeonholes: “Bodies of Water,” “Summer Dresses”
Plant-Human Quarterly: “Carolina Thistle”
Plume: “Nautilus: An Ode”
Rappahannock Review: “Sediment”
Rat's Ass Review: “Orionids, Field Report”

River Heron Review: "My Mother Kept Saying Azaleas"
San Pedro River Review: "A Singing Bowl"
Shō Poetry Journal: "Ode to the Broken"
Shut Down Strangers and Hot Rod Angels (Bone & Ink Press, 2019): "Baby Teeth"
Susurrus: A Literary Arts Magazine of the American South: "Wild Violets"
SWING: "Clutch"
Thimble: "Migration"
Whale Road Review: "Night, South Alabama, No Regrets," "Punctuation"

Personal Acknowledgments

Thank you, Hayley Mitchell Haugen, Founding Editor of Sheila-Na-Gig Editions, for belief in this work and infinite patience with me.

My gratitude, also—

To dear readers, friends, and mentors whose encouragement for over 35 years has been crucial: Robert G. Benson, William E. Clarkson, Mary Floyd-Wilson, Leslie Haynes, Kathryn B. McKee, Jennifer Davis Michael, Gerald L. Smith, and Mary Wheeling;

To Abbie Kiefer and Koss La for their timely friendships and beautiful words on this chapbook's behalf;

To poets in whose workshops some of these ideas emerged and for their insightful feedback: Jose Hernandez Diaz, Alina Stefanesçu, Sarah Ann Winn, and Shannon K. Winston;

To my virtual literary community, especially April Bradley, Romana Iorga, and Melissa Ostrom;

To Amy Aberg McLelland, pianist and composer, who commissioned one of these poems for her original chamber music concert;

To Joseph Arthur Johnson, Sr. (1961-2025), whose perennial question to me was: "when is the book coming out?" Oh, how I wish you were here to see it, Joe.

To Peter McPherson, for those conversations about geese;

To Linda Wagner-Martin, for giving me a place to live on short notice and slipping poetry under my door during my fugitive days forever ago;

To my in-laws, for cheering me on and being my family-of-love;

To Binx, "the hero dog," who thinks he's my guardian angel and well may be, and the cats, Greta and Fergus, for daily reminders that chaos can be creative;

To Will, my partner-in-everything, without whom I'd be adrift (words will never be enough);

To our grown "boyos," Walker and Colin, sweetly my biggest fans, our most precious creations.

In gratitude for and in memory of
my mother Barbara (1932-2024)
and father George (1932-2013)

For my lodestars, WMP II, WWP, & CTP

Contents

Ode to the Broken

Paintings and photographs of girls
with daffodils, their pre-Raphaelite

dresses & tresses, scalloped edges,
all Ophelia-like with frilly garlands

of flowers—I love their soft eyes
& yearning gazes even as I break

away from maidens. At the bus stop
the old woman reminds me of a blue

heron I saw once with a useless wing,
shaggy, carbon-shale, raggedy shawl—

like anyone off balance using a half-
open umbrella as walking stick or prop,

brokenly beautiful. To any & all creatures
who feel useless, forgotten—the hunched,

torn, word-ripped, silenced who sting
from open-handed slaps of loss, startle

at the hawk's screeching cry, the rabbit's
scream, I gravitate toward your gravitas,

fall headlong into your caves, mine
the darkness with you, our fevered eyes

casting beams just wide enough
to illuminate the way forward & out

of peril. I follow the rat's nest of hair
on the back of your head like it's a halo

of curls, your limping gait like it's flying.

Summer Dresses

> "I was much farther out than you thought
> And not waving but drowning."
> —Stevie Smith

One summer I watched my next-door neighbor string wash on the line. Clothespins looked awkward in her fingers. She pinched at collars; the shoulders kept slipping like she was wrestling with a ghost. The wet cloth tugged the line down like one demand after another. I heard voices rise from open windows. Her husband yelled over the fence at my dog when he barked, *shut up shut up* SHUT UP.

When my husband screamed like that, my dog jumped through our storm door to get to me, shattering glass. So much yelling, inside or out, shards of words on the floor, in his fur, in the air. I moved into the guest room after waking to unwelcome hands and breath. I suffocated long after I pulled away. I drank too much red wine which stained my lips, occasionally my shirt, the pages of my books. I would leave soon.

From the garden, I could see over the fence to her yard. The lawn looked scalped, dry, mown too closely. No rain for months. My dog came to me from behind the shed, carrying his tennis ball, tongue lolling. When he reached me, I knew no ball was in his mouth, his cheek so swollen it bulged, warm to the touch. Snake bite. I drove to the vet, where the dog got fluids, an antibiotic shot. Snakes were out, they said, looking for water.

Every day my neighbor hung the clothes, and I watched from a distance. I remember how everything seemed bodiless and strung up, unoccupied, my mind a blank. One late afternoon, a storm came quickly, finally rain. I watched her trying to retrieve the shirts blowing wildly in the wind, sleeves slapping her face. At dusk, while picking tomatoes, I saw her through her kitchen window, mostly just her face and arms as she washed dishes, the rest of her out of the window's frame, a humid mist between us. A white plate rose and fell into view, her hands lost one at a time in the water as she rinsed. She stopped and looked out once, maybe in my direction, maybe broken.

We never spoke, even when I moved out, my clothes haphazard on hangers, my milk crates of books thrown hurriedly into my car. Did she see me go, wonder why, already know, wish she could, too? I took my dog. I forgot the earrings my now-dead father gave me, tiny emeralds. I still dream about whole days billowing up against the sky, sleeveless summer dresses empty and waving. Or did we tie enough sheets together to make a giant white balloon? Take the basket I used to gather tomatoes and string it up with shirtsleeves? Hot air parachute over the fields squared below like quilts, the lowing sounds of cattle ooh-ing and ah-ing our ascent? *Look up*, we'd cry to everyone below. *Look up.* LOOK UP.

Dizzy

As a child, I’d sneak out to the flat rock
dampened by rain, fingerprinted
by fossil whorls, where on my back
I'd watch the sky until my father called.

Now, no one calls—
I wait, looking up at the cat’s yellow eyes
shining down from the redbud tree.
One, two, three stars fall. I am dizzy
from the height of things around me.

Geminids, Field Report

I'm in four layers plus a hooded cloak
and scarf, blankets under and over me.

I'm only held to earth by down and wool,
pulled improbably to cold. In my pocket,

my phone rests against my chest so I won't
get lost in time. My dog's my only company

but for falling stars. The ninth is the brightest
I've ever seen, trailing long in low humidity.

The wind gathers itself distantly, preparing
to roll through. I hear it sighing over bare

branches, feel it cooling my face, breathing
over my breath, my halo, clouding the dark.

This is how it feels to lie down in a field.
This is how it feels to have dirt at my back,

for my legs to tighten along their length
and cinch me to this place, hamstring catch,

knot, cramp. I am muscle. I am spine and eyes.
I am open to perimeters. A train whistle circles

me like an echo. I smell woodsmoke, hear the dog
close in the leaves, then feel his cold nose

dot my cheek while a car without a muffler
makes a distant roar somewhere over the ridge.

Above is one bright blinking plane.
The sky is dropping debris, iron-nickel

silicates, shiny trash, ejected bits of comets,
rejected super-heated streaks of speed. Stopped

by all the light, I feel my heart skip its beat, valve
flap its stubborn parachute, lag, and murmur

a syncopated pulse that fills my ears like the ocean
in a shell. Why do I think I can hold myself still
as blood lapses backwards, while the planets reel?

Nautilus: An Ode

"Wrecked is the ship of pearl!"
—Oliver Wendell Holmes

I fantasize about inhabiting a nautilus, how each chamber
is bigger than the last, how the shell, when seawater
leaves a chamber, achieves
weightlessness,

how I could put down barriers like the creature,
how unoccupied spaces would grow, or how, in buoyant
separate rooms, we could find ourselves again
floating,

but we were so dissimilar in our turning, spiraling
away, so I have left you behind, wall by wall.
(No need to spin back to our spira mirabilis.)
At great
depths,

the shell implodes: I'm not going any deeper.
Inside now I, too, am nacre, mother
of pearl. Even if I crack, I isolate the fissure.
That's how I could outgrow a shell, crawl its corridors,

feel my way through the smooth walls until suddenly—
light

(I am defenseless, but I am no longer inhabiting dread.)

Through a Quantum Flute

Predict only probabilities for the possible
sounds like a motto I should adopt. We say
"no wonder," but I am all wonder. If a qubit

can be both 0 and 1, then why can't we be solo
and together, or two places at a time, like
loneliness is everywhere in the crowded faces

at Starbucks or on the dance floor? Maybe I settle
for the smallest particle of anything. My palm holds
pond water as a trickle, emptying, but what if

tardigrades linger in the algae, clinging
to my fingers? What if that tardigrade became
tun beyond apocalypse, returned, itself,

plumped, moss-hungry? What of the narwhal
in danger that can freeze and flee, its heart rate
dropping like a rock while diving deep? (Intense

exertion should mean rocketing hearts, not
slowed ones, even in the coldest seas.) These
possibilities persist in contradiction. I hear

a crescendo of Debussy or birdsong, notes, lost
words trebling to a tipping point. It's a relief
to know the earth rotates absent my awareness,

that I have no idea what's happening in space
despite naming five things I can hear or four
I can see, filling up my diaphragm, counting

breaths, while you orbit, withhold. Here's how
to make particles of light talk to each other: play
them through a quantum flute where wavelengths

of photons wander. I will pass by,
pass through, into unmeasured air.

A Singing Bowl

> "That scraping of iron on iron when the wind
> rises, what is it?"
>
> —"Nocturne" Li-Young Lee

The question may seem open ended,
but something always answers, demands
something that doesn't love hard earth
pushing back shovel that gives of rust
on snow, ferric and bleak, in some cold
          excavation

dug deft-handedly to find what's misplaced
under thawed then re-frozen ground,
mud-rivulets, all crenellated, crowning,
until their tiny battlements come toppling
down, undefended, metal-struck,
          blade-on.

The sound of me unlocking
          a hold,
blood-taste of biting my lip, digging.

A lost wedding band, too loose, troweled-
over in the dirt, glints like the edge
of a tiny bowl. I imagine it full
of unsentimental, stainless sky
          as it sings.

Fugue State

She plays in the key of forgetting. Forgetting, she loses locale, landmarks. Landmarks wander in her mind. Her mind becomes an antic character. An antic character will wonder. Wonder is the destination, unmapped. Unmapped, her trip takes an unexpected turn. Turn loops past the gas station & church. Church reminds her of repentance, an altar. An altar takes shape in her mind like matter. Matter becomes quark, atom, & particle. Particle reminds her of clavicle. Clavicle curves, a bone at the base of throat. Throat opens to voice & air & words. Words may lie because nothing is as it seems. It seems that she is losing her mind. Her mind rounds a corner and runs into a door. A door swings, creaking, hinges into the cerebellum. The cerebellum rests under occipital & temporal. Temporal suggests time, which the eye meets, open. Open, she tiptoes in the vestibular corridors, hearing chimes. Chimes say the clock strikes down the hall. The hall is the vestibule where she waits for language. Language bears the thrum that she cups in her hands. Her hands open & memories fly out like birds. Birds always know where they are going. Going, she hangs her sorrows on a hook in the hall where they jangle, like keys, until she returns.

Telltales

It was the V that undid her.
When geese flew overhead,

Pete's mother used to cry.
She loved that no one bird

was strongest, how they alternate
the lead, switching places

as they tire. She missed
that pull of love, mourned

what she no longer had, the way
we do when we love most

what we lack when our timing's
off. Geese keep good time.

Trailing birds sync their wings
for free lift, trace the exact path

as the wing in front. The flock
evades downdrafts on purpose,

tracks uplifting currents. There's
a photograph of Pete's mother

and her sister circa 1942 aboard
a sailboat in the Charleston harbor

after their father left the Navy.
They're standing one in front

of the other, almost shoulder
to shoulder, looking fearlessly ahead.

Pete says most of his mother's past
otherwise is a mystery to him.

He knows that she was born in Manila,
always felt a bit displaced.

I haven't seen Pete since the 80's.
We've both lost friends since then.

By now, we know even families
are rarely aligned to each other's

movements, that we can't count on eddies
ahead to lift us into some fresh wash

of air—and why Pete's mother
was wistful in the birds' wake.

I imagine her on the old sailboat,
feathering through her teens

with her eyes on the yarn
of the telltales, waiting

for invisible wind.

Song for Cello & Girlhood

I rest my thoughts on the idea of your slender neck,
think of words that don't caress:
violent, vitriol, until I get
to violet, purpling to faded armchair
velvet, viol of the arm, low
notes rendered—no wolf tone howl but such sounds
your hollow body makes—mellifluous,
through ribs & catgut & shapes that draw air,
so that I, listening, forget to breathe
until my lungs take in what's trembling through
an open window at twilight just when
the coyotes offer their vibrato
& bravado: a girl two doors over
practicing for high school orchestra,
filling the air with her broken chords,
sighing September, as she drags her bow
across strings, solo—the perfect wail
of being seventeen, & I want to save her.

Pantoum Composed of Lines After Paintings of Girls

The girl I left behind me is not
the same; one hand parts the curtain.
She shifts her gaze past the promontory toward
the sea. Her face and the moon are

the same. One hand parts the curtain.
In the other, she holds a letter—no, a balloon,
the sea. Her face and the moon are
reflections that flood the interior.

In her other life, she holds a letter—no, a balloon
she releases to the sky like a note of air,
a reflection that floods her interior
rooms with words and music. Practice interrupted,

she releases to the sky like a note of air
all that kept her tethered to other views,
rooms with words and music; practice interrupted,
herself as object, study, story. Everything,

all that kept her tethered to other views,
she shifts. She gazes past the promontory toward
herself: subject, student, story, everything
the girl I left behind me was not.

Polymorphous Pigeon in the Art Museum

One afternoon I saw a homing pigeon studying a painting, then preening. I suppose he entered the museum the same way birds enter malls or airports. His feathers shimmered like colors in the frames, everything awash in blues and greens. Most people believe that pigeons are not as smart as crows or blue jays. Like doves, they seem oblivious, flocking, food-focused, a nuisance.

There's always more than meets the eye: A single vaned feather is composed of interlocking filaments, barbule, nanostructure, melanosomes. In 1918 a pigeon named Cher Ami carried a message for a U.S. Battalion trapped behind German lines before being shot right out of the sky, miraculously returning to headquarters though wounded.

Pigeons may not know the word "polymorphous," but they can distinguish between classes of beings, between pigeon and person, between Monet and Picasso or Bach and Stravinsky. It's true. My museum companion preferred Monet to Delacroix and Delacroix to Cezanne, was known to react to Picasso's abstract images. *Water Lilies-Morning, Still Life with Lobster, The Large Bathers,* and *Weeping Woman* were his favorite paintings. I can only guess why. Water is compound. Stark figures. Tableaux. Uneven eyes and lines, greens, yellows, anguished mouth, inscrutable expressions. Everything more than it seems.

This bird didn't steal Picasso's painting (though he may have tipped off the police with a note). He didn't shy away from suffering or brokenness, saw himself in Monet's colors, stepped right through the museum door the way I'd like to step through the frame, trace brush strokes into sky, feel buoyance in water.

Compassion might float: iridescent, mirrored. A pigeon's feathers gleam.

Migration

Everyone talks about October light as if
        it's a singularity, but light is
a variable one month can't contain. Light is
        a life story in which the world
glances through space while the last
        hummingbirds cut the air with delicate
precision & tulip poplars are on the wing,
        their leaves & their leavings, & once,
looking up, I saw birds impossibly
        high in a broken line (if pattern could be
syncopated), bird by bird in staggered sequence:
        sandhill cranes, which explains the length
of their passing ghostlike above, long silhouettes
        in & out of clouds, reminding me
how my mother dappled in & out of my view—
        after her diagnosis, metastasis, we were farther
than a wingspan apart even when I was right
        next to her bedside while nothing changed
but everything. I hold light more tenderly now,
        knowing how it goes.

Is there anything bluer

than twilight? Nothing beckons like the liminal. Even the grass looks like the sea where she could trail bioluminescent fingers, fireflies afloat. They *sink and rise and sink and rise and sink again.* She is always after the night, its edges so beautiful in their blurring, and how a lamp somewhere glows through a pane while curtains fall over all her days. Something is off plumb in her mind, out of true; she says the house is still there across the yard. She says she can still see it from her window. *I was told to look for blue,* where I'd find her,

> and each time she said,
> "remind me when we get there,"
> I would know to look.

Punctuation

From the window, she watches her son make a snow angel. His little arms outstretched, arcing the snow into wings, his puffy red coat like a puckered scar on the snow. The branches at the yard's edge fray to the ground like fingers trailing. They remind her of a childhood game, silly, strangely intimate: *X marks the spot with a line and a dot and a dash-dash-dash and a b-i-g question mark,* someone writing on her arm with a fingertip. Trying to decipher the symbols through touch was strangely hard, like watching invisible ink fade, one shape eliding with another. *Cool breeze* prefaced breath on her neck that always made her shiver. Then her friend would *crack an egg* on her head, fingers pulling through her hair down shoulder blades to vertebrae to rib cage, circles *up and down and all the way around* as they giggled. It was about that age that she tried to shake snow from a cedar tree, pulling the lowest branch with her mittened hands. She remembers how suddenly it slipped her grasp and thrashed back icy and sharp into one eye, how that eye wept for days. Now she watches the snow angel's legs sweep back and forth until the ground shows, bits of mud streaking here and there like broken parentheses on paper. Then he lies so still that he must be holding his breath; she sees the exhalation when it marks the air, floats, suspends for a second, disappears. When he comes inside, he says he can't feel his fingers and starts to cry as they tingle and burn. *Why are your eyes watering?* he asks her through his tears as she helps him pull his wet sleeves one by one from each arm, the puddles beneath them on the floor circling deeper and wider.

I Will Hunger

> "the wind, the wind, / the heavenly child"
>
> —"Hansel and Gretel"

> "Don't confuse hunger with greed;
> And don't wait until you are dead."
>
> —Ruth Stone, "Advice"

All paths lead toward hunger.
Hunger is a snarling wolf,
a house of confection,
the sweet that rots the tooth,
the cramp that drowns her,
an ogre, an ache in the voice
of a mother, stepmother, witch.
They say to the children,
do not stray off the path,
do not ask for anything.

In her small hands, hunger
dissolves like sugar; in his,
a breadcrumb turns to dust,
a brittle measure, poof! Lost.
A crumbling map, a stone
to fill up the wolf. Pebbles
like coals in a stove turn
to cinder, vanish. Fingers
pinch the fat; fat sizzles.

Don't follow the forest
trail to a thicket of need
where briars catch, pull
at hair, scratch the skin,
strip tenderloins of flesh.
Berries burst. Blood attracts
the ravenous creatures

in the hollows and houses.
The maw is the mother, her
mouth, the oven, the hope
that appetite leaves you
gaping, wild, sated.

And the mother
swallows nothing but her
tongue, her words ash on
a cigarette's tip; she stands
up straight, her pencil skirt tight
around her waist; high heels make
her taller. She wears them to look
slimmer, define her calves, counts
calories heart by heart, handful
by handful, until she disappears
into the wind, the wind.

Night, South Alabama, No Regrets

In ragged blouses and shorts that sagged, we summer children scattered and caught what we could. The smallest girl always dragged her feet. Her hand in mine was wet with fear of dark, but I let go to race you; you won as usual. I showed off my newest scar, where the briar caught my knee. You said you couldn't see anything.

It was always too dark to play, not dark enough to sleep.

Inside, the cot stretched long and white down the living room made warm by furniture, breath, and when it was cold, furnace heat. On holidays, family overflow nudged the younger out; we winter children ate and slept on the edges, kitchens, porches, roll-a-way beds, dim spaces lit by portable heaters. When the cot was mine, I couldn't help but hear the older men in the same room talk softly of hunting grounds and ponds filled with bass and bream.

It was always too dark to play, not dark enough to sleep.

I knew you would get up at dawn to go with them while I would pretend to sleep, warm and restless under a quilt. One uncle told a story about seeing a bear outside his house––"as close as you are to me," he said—leading her half-grown cubs past the barn toward the trees. Every scrape or scratch of branch against screen made my nerves run. I wished I'd let the smallest girl hold my hand just that once.

It was always too dark to play, not dark enough to sleep.

When I finally dreamed, a great mother bear came to the door. I ran by myself into the universe, my stride suddenly ten feet long, and she led me out among the stars where we stretched, suspended,

our own constellation.

Orionids, Field Report

It's not really that cold.
I see the first before I'm even settled.
I'm on my back in the brittle grass
before the next four fall. Night noises
fall around me. My dog's face hovers
over mine. Sometimes all I see is his chin,
silhouetted. Colder now that I'm still,
I start count, as if by that act I summon
the stars, and I'm up to ten when I hear the train
whistle a low wail that fades, lonesome
in the distance, then coyotes, a few yips,
then howls, until my dog howls along
with either the train or them. It doesn't matter.
I'm not sure which is closer.
His breath is a plume in the dark;
then he's gone across the field, and I hope
for one more, repeating the mantra to myself
one more, one more, one more
until that star streaks across the sky, trailing
light, faint and quick. There. Not there.
Maybe I conjured the vision, my eyes watering,
my face now cold, my back stiff on the ground.
I think to myself: I am rigid like a corpse.
The dog checks on me, warm breath coming back.
It's possible to be still in a turning world,
to let the dark be dark,
the cold be cold,
the sky be what it is,
the stars what they are
or once were.

I Used to Be

A torrent of storm, a craze of sound, a field.
A barefoot girl surprised by a sudden flood.
Steel clouds, darkening sky, a yield to wind.
The dash through, the here, the gone.
June skies breaking. Drenched. Waist-deep.
Flash of light. Steaming grass.
Something that opens, slips by,
disappears in the rain like a dream.

Driving Rain

The last thing I want when driving is the rain driving, too. The phrase is perfect. The rain drives around & over us, driving the point home that we may never get there, constant percussion a wordless refrain the tires keep trying to shush, relentless glare on the windshield, unexpected splash on the left from a car out of nowhere already out of sight again, hydroplane on the right in invisible water pooled by the shoulder—that slip like a belt's lurch & catch that's hard to describe when you know immediately but still too late that you've lost purchase & control, left the ground for an instant / hovered / defied gravity but succumbed again like getting your breath knocked out of you for the first time & how I remember, when he was little, my son said rain sounds made him feel cozy during road trips—I think of him dozing behind me & feeling safe while the strain of seeing ahead made me afraid to blink & how I'd get inexplicably attached to the taillights of a semi as if the glow could tow us forward, magical thinking, the rain driving me mad for a minute, crazed to get him safely where we were going / where he is going / & how I can't ever really get him beyond all of the hazards.

Bodies of Water

At dock's edge, where the lake lengthened out its quiet dark,
buoys rocked in the *lap-lap-lap* of invisible currents, and the
unseen made us tremble, the hair rising on our arms, we
pulled at hems and stubborn sleeves in haste. Racing the
storm, we slipped shivering into water as blue gray as slate,
shallower than we thought—where

> the bottom shifted below us. I cut my foot on glass
> half buried in the silt, tilted back to float and look,
> only my toes surfacing, felt the guilt only a 13-year-
> old good girl would feel for sneaking out at camp.
> The cut was white at its edges. My foot looked
> strange, wrinkled, as detached as someone else's.
> Blood bloomed like a time-lapsed flower. I dove
> down, found the fragment of glass that turned
> emerald-dark in the cloud break under a sliver of
> moon—

such opaque, curved offerings. When I swam out to you, the
skin around my cut rippled like a fragile gill reminding me
to breathe. We couldn't stay long, our legs barely touching
under water. Someone was calling *time to get back*. We kicked
to the dock. You said into my ear, *imagine: your cut will scar
like a sliver of moon*. Then under my feet, wet boards steamed.
Another girl slipped and laughed. The wind picked up a
waft of pine, the storm closer, closing in. Suddenly scared of
getting caught, we were only legs and arms, the slipping
touch of fingers to back, the brush of someone's hair,
whispers

> and fear. So hard to pull at clothes wet from
> splashes, denim clinging to skin. After all that
> careless touching, we were suddenly modest and
> shy. The pines also whispered as we made our way
> back, the paths of straw so soft, my foot didn't hurt

in those steps away from skinny-dipping secrets and
touches, from our selves then, such tenderness like
ghosts walking beside us. On the last night we
returned to the lake, made cardboard boats, pressed
candles on with melted wax, burned our fingers as
we lit the wicks and set them all afloat—small
flames aloft on nothing more than layered paper
rocked by the mouths

of minnows. Unsteady light flickered around our faces each
time a match was struck. Mist rose off the lake, and we were
rising, falling, too, the dock creaking. We tasted June as a
coin on the tongue, as ferric as bronze or blood. Fugitive
communion in memory of bodies we didn't think we'd lose.
Selves who'd never be as intimate with each other again.
Invisible currents carrying everything where the moon
whispered mouths away. A kiss. A scar.

How Lost Words Haunt Like Wings Behind Glass

(a cento)

The ghost girl / makes no noise,
a restless ghost in a house the wind owns;
there was no fanfare no terror only a blue silhouette
forever in your house, in your garden, in corridors,
        our own omissions in a room;
she will spend all day counting their shadows like stitches
opening, and ghost-
like butterflies, errant and flamboyant,
unanswered messages like ghosts in the throat
the way a lost / word / will come back / unbidden
        —with its *no one* without its I—
glass, ghostly opposition, vowel
that I would be—dryadic, gothic, fanatic against
a spirit-lantern to spin shapes inside:
        one need not be a chamber to be haunted,
only myself. You see, I was the ghost:
        there's no such thing /   as an unhaunted house.

Baby Teeth

no one thought to look beneath the stacks
of magazines, behind the rows of nail polish
in your bedroom for clues
a diary, a photograph, love letters
a word collage, that dried up corsage

They could've taken a good look around.

the tires serenaded as you slipped out
stealing along the edge of trees to the road
watching for the headlights on, then off,
the shiver down your back
your hair tangled from running

At first it was exactly like you pictured.

you were sliding into the car
catching your purse strap on the door
your legs sticking to the vinyl seats
you were laughing
his hand along your arm, a thrill
wheels slipping on the gravel road
going nowhere but places too well-known

All you'd wanted to do was dance.

empty storefronts at dawn, "for lease"
in dirty windows, gas stations and dust
the Buick's steering loose on the turns
when you'd gone too far to look back

You should've taken a good look around.

later with the ring tight
on your finger in the summer heat

you remembered the string
of baby teeth your father kept
in a Shaker box of cherry wood
its swallowtails curling around
the sides and how neatly the lid
fit and inside a map of yourself
should you become lost or dead

Those little pearls of goodbyes.

Sediment

If you hear anything over
          and over again,
it's going to make a dent
          like water into rock.

That's how people get
          cavernous,
one too many times
          called worthless

in hollow love.
          Picture limestone.
You know how it softens,
          gives way to sediment,

allows whole epochs
          to slide by and through.
That's how ages go. Slowly.
          That's how time stretches out.

That's why when the first drop
          falls, you must take note.
Otherwise, your surfaces erode;
          all that debris will wear you down.

You'll become just another
          system of caves where more
and more people get lost.
          That's why you must get out.

Clutch

Your car wouldn't go into reverse.
It was a stick shift, the kind I learned
on in driver's ed. Always at an angle,
a ruby slash against the black top
like lipstick smeared on a cup, a missed
kiss. You always took up two spaces,
which pissed people off. You had
to park it that way so you could get out.
That summer I saw your red Mustang
everywhere, idling in parking lots
by the city pool, air chlorine-thick,
at the drive-in on humid nights away
from everyone else, shimmering like
asphalt. I still picture you leaning against
it, shirtless, careful not to let your skin
touch metal. Late 70s. Your hair sun-
bleached, stick-straight. You had
a swimmer's body, broad shoulders,
but you were short, so you laughed
about it, like how you couldn't afford
to fix your car, like the speed you took
so you could get up for your day job.
Sometimes you asked me to call at 5:00 a.m.
I'd sneak down to the basement
so my father wouldn't hear me.
You were always awake already. I think
you liked to hear my voice first thing.
Tied to the wall, the phone cord coiled
around my fingers, I whispered to you.
When we got off work, we'd meet
at the public pool before it closed.
I'd lie on one side & you on the other,
our faces almost touching at the deep
end corner. Sometimes you slept. I'd
count freckles on your cheeks. Over

the chain link fence, I could see the Mustang
like a guardian. Like a guardian angle,
we'd laugh. I always knew you were going.
I wanted you to get out, away from
the house where your mother hoarded
cats & newspapers. I never forgot what
you told me about taking care of my car.
"Don't let your clutch go bad," you said—
"it won't decouple properly—
it will seize everything up."

Matters as Simple as Quantum Mechanics

Does it matter if a period is placed just so,
like a gentle hand against a lover's back?

Language has its own mechanics with grammar
exacting its rules; "composition" could include

almost anything—music, quartz, or quark. And
mechanics toil over engines or inventions, examine

clutches, lubrication, bearings, couplings, reliability
or other such parts of machinery, well-oiled, steeled

up, words also describing lovers at their best, or worst.
Forever fails as often as physicists obsess over light

and colliders, ionize vapor in cloud chambers, track
cosmic rays. Polarities may complicate matters

as simple as attraction. The right sign can fix
a splice or run-on, stop a runaway train or person,

anyone leaving or decoupling because parts froze
or engines stopped, and words cross over

lines of subject matter in grand weirdness,
can wound or soothe. No interpretation exiled,

one word here means another there, like a miracle—
or curse—as parts shake loose, muon or noun,

Higgs boson or fiery verb, dangling modifiers.
Is the culprit of bad mechanics "love,"

the variable by which language veers, absent
bearing (like particles run amok, driven by magnetism),

and splits into sentiments too heavy to parse
in a parsec lengthening into space, leaving fragments

in the wake of a promise up to a vanishing point?
Two bodies, forever entangled, the end.

You Only Ghosted Me in Your Head

That heaviness on my eye
is really the moon at three a.m.,
bright afterimage all I can see—

your eclipse: my provision
for travel. It seems little evidence
exists for an obol on the eyelids

in antiquity, anyway. No need
for coins to ransom me from caverns
of your dead. I told you once:

distance could be metaphorical,
which of course you misunderstood,
how stopped up are the spaces

between words, what with pride
choking your mouth, how ferric
the taste of blood when I bit

my lip to keep from saying
what I thought—now I take
your lack of depth into account,

plumb whatever sea floor the night
sky is, as if it could be measured
from the underworld that is yours.

No boat ferries me from you:
no telling how far I've gone. I'm not
saying a word. But I won't be there

this time, a hand at shore. Not that
I'm expecting you, the respect
I might have deserved. Instead,

I've taken the screech owls' rippled
cries for a ride at the last minute,
accepted the trill of calls in the dark

as my destination, my *viaticum,*
their holy whinnying one to another
from tree to tree, a kind of joy.

Unreliable Narratives [how to let a body]

As 70s teens watching Bond films
with obvious villains & femmes fatales,
we must have been so confused. Shame

waited on us at our heels: name-
calling in the early 80s, when a girl
could be a "slut" in college by rumor

alone, not to mention, in slasher-
films, that terrible slit was for throats,
& who died first? We knew.

But we also could be "frigid" just
by refusing to be groped. Some
narratives were not clear despite

our childhood memories of maidens
kissed after poisoned apples, fragile
slippers, deep sleeps, magic mirrors.

Before cartoon in myth & lore,
a mermaid could be silenced, name-less,
allow a sea-witch to cut out her tongue,

agree to swallow potion to be human,
or at least grow legs pierced by sword-
like pain when she walked—all for love.

Even Ariel, swaddled almost to her cleavage
in scales, still—from her open throat,
oh, how she sang until her voice's theft,

& that's the question: how to enthrall,
be part-this, part-that, chimera, half-
fish or -bird, siren, alluring, dangerous

(back to femme fatale), how to say what must
be said, un-binary the labels, keep a story
liminal—as changeable as the sea—skirmish

possible endings (careless slip of word,
drowning, cleft of knife), how to let
a body glimmer, surface, float, fly—   be.

Lioness

I think about how cats drape themselves over
furniture, loose and lissome and lithe, boneless almost,
and how I could not arrange myself just so if I tried, not

my body, unless deliberately posed by an artist:
barely breathing, arm thrown overhead as if with abandon,
a nude, an odalisque, trying to occupy a form that I am not,

that is—svelte, smooth, and impervious to gravity's
pull. I do know how it is to be directed to hold still, bare
breast pressed on dark plates by a mammographer.

She's taped my surgical scar with an X so it won't
interfere with a clear image. Now hold your breath,
she says, then okay: . . .   breathe.

The instructions make me breathless
though I know they're coming. I'm a gasp
waiting to happen on a cold metal slab.

A gloved hand rearranges me again. Lean in, forward,
but not *that* far. My elbow higher on the frame, my chin up
more. I am what is squeezed, clamped, irradiated,

imaged, screened, staged, this mammalian me, past
childbearing. My inhalations so deep they fill
my belly like a balloon, I may rise soon despite

the sagging down, except my mind is fun-house mirror;
through wide angle lens like a fish or pinhole distortions,
my eye sees. I wind the clinic halls again, looking

for the right door, horror-movie imaginings of the wrong
one, terror not of what I might find but of what might
be found in me. Back in the dressing room, shedding robe

to floor, I dress, dare myself, level my gaze like a lioness,
amber-glow-steady; I saunter to check out, low-slung,
stealth-hipped, and fierce, my feet like velvet paws.

If I could arrange myself like that under
open-skied savanna, without before or after,
I would sway free of days, my breath a roar.

After the Anniversary Party for the Feathery Woman & Blindfolded Man

No one thought they'd make it this long, a union founded on deceit and whimsy, or so the rumors went. But they had a portable dance floor, a party tent, a clearing in the middle of nowhere, conductor in tails and top hat waving his hands madly. A full orchestra took turns playing with a blues band from Memphis. Wind whipped the leaves around. Her feathers were streaked with gray. On the man's brow, lines ran more deeply where cloth covered his eyes. For fun, she'd had her wedding gown made into a boa draped now over her shoulders, feathering more. His blindfold looked exactly the same. The atmosphere was strangely dark yet effervescent, with champagne and Jell-O shots served in acorn cupules. Guests, sweet and gracious during the toasts, were awkwardly uninhibited. Then, the music stopped. We received small silver flashlights as favors so we could find our way out of the forest. We'd danced so long even the trees were tired of swaying. So much mud on my heels that I slipped them off, my dress hem snagged, sodden with dew, a train of green. When the party ends, even the air quiets, blows wide open, empty as a sleeve. For days, leaves trailed me; pine needles dropped from my hair; acorns fell from my pockets. I wore loneliness like a cloak over my wings.

Clef

Try to stay level while the world falls
away. Try to find the notes like steps

on a steep path. Balance as if you're
a clavicle. Pretend you are the cliff,

primordial & still—or a clavichord
for quiet practice, string by string

over a bridge. The life you suspend
is your own, vertebra by vertebra

holding up. Inside our bones,
tissue more porous than limestone,

latticework for marrow. Imagine
the staff to which the notes cling,

one tritone interval drawing suspense
out. No loss is minor. We lean toward

resolution. What is always behind
the door at the top of the stairs

is love. Even though we all know
the end, we stave off what we can.

What I'm trying to say is
how brave:

we cleave anyway.

Carolina Thistle

I find the prickly foliage kindred, the thistle
in its proliferating. My brittle thoughts

inadequate at grief's threshold, I let spines
grow unhindered from the base floret

by the porch where I can see the plant,
not anticipating, exactly, what I want.

I know the purplish flowers go to seed,
fritillaries love its nectar, monarchs might

flock, but I understood the thistle's
offering best when wiry stems unclasped,

releasing downy wisps to sail on breezes.
When a hummingbird's wing cut the air

with a whir, late migration, I looked up.
All I could picture was my mother's white

hair barely covering her skull, a fine tonsure,
and think of cells gone rogue. What

is breath but everything? Then suddenly:
brilliance, goldfinches flashing on spent

blooms in the breeze, feasting. Why can't
we go like that? Rollicking and sated,

gorgeous, unexpected guests as wind
scatters our tendrils behind like promises,

the only spreading: more flowers.

Wild Violets

Tiptoe past the tall, silent jars of preserved
pickles, beans, tomatoes, and peaches that sink

arrested in their clove-redolent peppercorn brines,
past the stolid wooden bowls of apples on the table,

and push the kitchen door out into April with me
where, before the first mow, the tiny violets

repeat themselves in spring babble, purple
white, yellow, blue, a mantra uttered, scattered

over verdant crowns. See how the veins mark
their petals in watercolor, as chaotic as aberrant

scans or EKG tremors of a galloping heart,
how the flowers arch like periwinkle shells,

two halves, butterfly wings. Their nonsense
is mine. I hold them in reserve, their silliness,

abandon, in my mind's eye (all aperture, iris-
wide, watery, a salty pool) where I float

from petal to petal, sipping sweetness as long
as I can, which is not long at all, some blade

as close as a blink, so the image must stay pulse
in the throat, memory, this purple flowering

its own spell: I give you . . .
violets, violets, violets.

Fugitive but Gorgeous

She thinks about all the ways that girls bleed while she follows the red dirt road to the pasture. Dust covers her bare feet because it is August and dry. She squeezes under the barbed wire fence. Brambles catch her legs; blood beads from ankle to shin. The scratches itch, so she wipes her leg distractedly, realizes the sting, licks her finger, tastes iron. Grounded by a root as white and hard as bone, the pokeweed is as tall as she remembered, stalks towering like in the fairy tale with the giant, a canopy overhead. She's after all the berries she can reach but not to eat. She crushes them until they explode like fireworks, purpling her hands. She tints her cheeks, her lips. Her mother won't let her wear makeup. She remembers her father telling her they call the plant "poke sallet," that sallet means cooked greens. Its berries are toxic, some say; others say a tonic, medicinal. She thinks about the girl in the Elvis song who was so hungry she ate a mess of the greens just to survive, so unlucky, her family in trouble. Did "Polk Salad Annie" ever eat the fruit, her arms ache from toting the stalks for miles? She will tell her mother it was an accident, the day she stained her shorts, her white cotton tee, anything she should not touch. She wipes her hands on her clothes, heads home just before sunset, paints herself into the horizon where magenta and lavender swirl in the sky.

Haunt Like This

Don't mind when beetles
swarm on summer nights.

Find a cicada's fragile hull
attached to tree bark by one

jointed leg, white strands
of old lungs still aloft

above shell spiracles. Watch
the June bug's iridescent green

zag a crazy line through
unmown grass. Want

to haunt like this. Without
question. Visibly. To be heard. No

second guessing. A hum,
vibrato, buzz. Trade

exuviae for air, claw
out with broken

fingernails, wings.

Undomesticated Ghosts

She leaves the sewing sisters inside with their baskets of endless yarns, the years winding around, threads keeping them tied to beds and kitchens, tiptoes past the sentinels of preserved tomatoes, beans, pickles, and peaches to the yard where the matriarch of the cats, her tail twitching in the dust, lies nursing her usual litter of too many kittens—always too many—and past the cornfield to the last barn at the woods' edge where the door is always ajar to the room where the sun slants between boards that do not quite fit together, and eyeholes in the wood reveal dust, motes of hay, where the contrast between the late fall burning sun and interior darkness requires her eyes to adjust to the sight of a grandmother leaning over a watering can as if divining something on that long-still stagnant surface which does not reflect her face but only her wavering as if she too is slipping, leaching away through the split sides of anything that can't contain it any longer than the barn can keep out rain splattering onto the swept patterns of dust on a floor where too many feet have come and gone without knowing why, shoes and souls.

•

She leaves the sewing sisters in the dust past the cornfield and the endless dark. There is only her wavering, ajar, the years winding around in swept patterns. She is divining something, nursing the split sides, always too many, keeping the barn out of the rain, leaning over the kittens and the beans, finding her way into the sky.

Mapping

A red dirt road led to my grandfather's pond—or to the top of the dovetailed dresser in my childhood bedroom, strange landscape where I kept the only arrowhead I've ever found, its chiseled edges so different from the buckeye I saved for luck, smooth like my river stones—all these hard things knocking against each other in a turtle shell, scraped clean, that my grandfather gave me when I didn't understand its emptiness meant death, or that the turkey tail feather he gave me, which I pretended was a quill, inked and storied with genetic code, was a lonely banded plume, tales long over, now stripped of bird where nests littered dust, where eggshell fragments (robin-blue) and mica shimmered next to the pink jewelry box filled with buttons, its tinny notes and plastic, spinning ballerina alien to me because I was more at home among the stranded and scavenged.

After my father died, I found my baby teeth swathed in a handkerchief in his chest of drawers like tiny pearls. In late fall, dry leaves would cover the clay-hard road so thickly that wind rustled a whisper buried in that hollowed-out terrain like a ghost. I don't even know if the pond is still there where I first learned to send a stone

skimming

as lightly as a feather over water.

The Deer Meat Becomes Hands

title from Linda Hogan's "Inside"
(for my father, 1932-2013)

        I keep
thinking of his hands,
how dexterous with splint
or needle. He could salve
a burn, stitch a tiny cut
so well with surgeon's skill
it would hardly scar, stave
off everything but death.
        I keep
thinking of his hands
deftly sectioning citrus
into ambrosia, how he cleaned a fish,
scales glittering on a summer afternoon,
sewed felt onto a holiday ornament, bent
a wooden split to weave a stool seat
or basket, made a tiny bird feeder
for a dollhouse.
        I keep
thinking of his hands
every time I use what he'd labored
over, preserved, squeezed, hulled,
peeled, skinned, or dressed
over cutting block or table:
key lime juice, pecans—the smallest
ones I'd ever seen—picked clean
from intricate shells, a pint
of leek and potato soup, packs
of venison parts: backstrap,
steaks, ground, dated, labeled.
        I keep
thinking of his hands
because I hadn't remembered

in grief's haze what was in the cooler
I brought back from Alabama.
He seemed to be almost wholly there.

My mother kept saying azaleas

(for my mother, 1932-2024)

when she meant the Lenten roses
she gave me from her garden: *Helleborus,*
perennial which propagates over time, takes
several years to bloom, is among the first
to show green shoots above decaying leaves
we've left alone. A dried hellebore bloom looks
like a face in a sepia photograph. *Hellebore*
makes me think of Cerberus, Orpheus, charms,
music, underworlds. Something we inherit,
don't want to forget, a name. Our mothers'
gardens are often plundered—so goes her last
breath

while my hellebores are full and white,
their carmen-centered petals ruffled
like old-fashioned petticoats; they flounce
their edges, hover over cold ground like ghosts.
I wish the breezes could infuse my mother's
lungs with air, her tumors shrink, her sight
return, or hearing, while I'm at it, be sensitive
enough to register spring peepers, their
incantations drifting over grass and clover
at dusk; her dying was not that tender,
but let her be as gently felt,
present

as darkness yields to white flowers,
as I remember her azaleas,
how pink their blooms like mouths.

Notes

The epigraph for "**Nautilus: An Ode**" (page 17) is from Oliver Wendell Holmes's "The Chambered Nautilus." This poem was inspired in part by my fascination with logarithmic spirals, a mathematical concept replicated in nature, including in the biological structure of mollusk shells. The phrase "spira mirabilis" used in the poem is Latin for "miraculous spiral," another name for this phenomenon given by Swiss mathematician Jacob Bernoulli. The poem references mollusks, which are able to repair their shells from the inside. A type of mollusk also related to octopi and squid, the nautilus is a soft-bodied cephalopod which inhabits its shell's largest chamber while expelling water through the other chambers that act like ballasts to control buoyancy and propel the nautilus through the sea. An actual nautilus does not outgrow its shell but rather creates new, larger spaces within it, walling off smaller chambers as it does. The inner layer of a nautilus shell, "nacre," is pearl-like in luster and iridescent—hence Holmes's reference to the "ship of pearl."

"**Through a Quantum Flute**" (page 18) borrows ideas from "UChicago Scientists Invent 'Quantum Flute' That Can Make Particles of Light Move Together" from the University of Chicago News website.

In nautical terms, "**Telltales**" (page 21) are bits of yarn or ribbon attached to sailboat riggings to indicate wind so sails can be adjusted accordingly, and "feathering" refers to adjusting propellers or sails to minimize drag or sailing upwind to reduce boat tipping or heel.

"**Pantoum Composed of Lines After Paintings of Girls**" (page 24) is after *The Girl I Left Behind Me* (Eastman Johnson, 1870-1875), *The Girl by the Window* (Edvard Munch, 1893), *Girl at a Window* (Salvador Dalí, c. 1925), *Girl Reading a Letter at an Open Window* (Johannes Vermeer, 1657-1659), *Girl Reading a*

Letter in an Interior (Peter Vilhelm Ilsted, 1908), *Balloon Girl* (Banksy, 2000s), *Girl Interrupted at Her Music* (Vermeer, 1658-1661).

"**Polymorphous Pigeon in the Art Museum**" (page 25) uses findings from S. Watanabe, J. Sakamoto, and M. Wakita's article, "Pigeons' discrimination of paintings by Monet and Picasso," *Journal of the Experimental Analysis of Behavior, 63,* 1995, 165-74. Regarding other references in the poem: Picasso's *The Weeping Woman* was stolen in 1986 from the National Gallery of Victoria in Australia but recovered undamaged in a railway station locker after police received an anonymous tip.

"**Is there anything bluer**" (page 27) is loosely after *remind me when we get there* (2022) and *The Deep End* (2023) by American artist Jeremy Miranda and borrows lines from Edna St. Vincent Millay's "Love is Not All, Sonnet XXX" and Carl Phillips' "Blue."

"**How Lost Words Haunt Like Wings Behind Glass**" (page 37) is a cento that uses lines from poems that reference spirits or haunted places: Rae Armentrout's "Unbidden," Charles Baudelaire's "Les Phares" ("The Beacons"), Lucie Brock-Broido's "How Can It Be I Am No Longer I," Andrea Cohen's "Gratitude," Emily Dickinson's "One Need Not Be a Chamber — to be Haunted," Sean Thomas Dougherty's "The Dead Are Everywhere Telling Us Things," Carolyn Forché's "Sequestered Writing," Cynthia Huntington's "Ghost," Elizabeth Jennings's "Ghosts" (a translation of Ferencz Győző's "Kísértetek"), Donika Kelly's "Sighting: Avalanche," Ben Lerner's "Meridian Response," Ada Limón's "Late Summer After a Panic Attack," Eric Pankey's "Restless Ghost," Ruben Quesada's "XI," Natalie Rose Richardson's "My Aunt's Angels," Brenna Twohy's "A Coworker Asks Me if I Am Sad, Still," and Mark Wunderlich's "Gone is Gone." Slashes denote line breaks in originals; italics and em dashes are original, not mine.

"**After the Anniversary Party for the Feathery Woman & Blindfolded Man**" (page 51) was inspired by an image in "Mistaken for Strangers," a song released by The National on the album *Boxer* (2007).

"**Clef**" (page 52) debuted as the shorter poem "Triple Clef" commissioned for *Glimpses of Grief and Glee,* a concert of original chamber music composed by Amy Aberg McLelland and performed February 07, 2021, at Independent Presbyterian Church, Birmingham, AL. One line is a slant nod to Flannery O'Connor's short story "The Life You Save May Be Your Own."

The song referenced in "**Fugitive but Gorgeous**" (page 55), "Polk Salad Annie," was written and recorded in 1968 by Tony Joe White and peaked at Number 8 on the *Billboard* Hot 100 in 1969, making it his biggest hit. In 1970, both Elvis Presley and Tom Jones covered the song. For more on poke sallet's culinary and medicinal properties, see "How did this Poisonous Plant Become One of the American South's Most Long-Standing Staples?" by Abby Carney, *Saveur*, 03, October 2019. Though initially bright and saturated, natural dyes, such as color rendered from pokeweed berries, are known as "fugitive" because they are not colorfast when exposed to factors such as sunlight, humidity, temperature, or time.

About the Author

Elinor Ann Walker's poems have been featured on *Verse Daily*, in several anthologies, and appear or are forthcoming in *AGNI, American Poetry Journal, Bayou Magazine, Bear Review, Nimrod International Journal, Plant-Human Quarterly, Plume, Poet Lore, Quarterly West, The Southern Review, Terrain,* and elsewhere. She holds a Ph.D. in English from the University of North Carolina-Chapel Hill, lives in the Appalachian foothills, and is on the poetry staff at *River Heron Review.* Winner of the 2024 Sheila-Na-Gig Editions First Chap Prize, *Fugitive but Gorgeous* is her first book. *Give Sorrow* (Whittle Micro-Press) is forthcoming. Find her online: https://elinorannwalker.com.

S
Sheila-Na-Gig Editions

www.ingramcontent.com/pod-product-compliance
Ingram Content Group UK Ltd.
Pitfield, Milton Keynes, MK11 3LW, UK
UKHW042012190726
13854UKWH00005B/2254